I0167528

Take Off
with
Airplane Science!

This course was written by
Naturally Curious Expert
Deborah McArthur

*Deborah is a science educator who loves connecting
others to the wonders of the physical and natural world.*

Printed by CreateSpace

ISBN 978-1-942403-09-8

www.benaturallycurious.com

Many activities in this book make use of printed materials. If you prefer not to cut them directly from this book, please visit the URL listed below and enter the code for a supplemental PDF containing all printable materials.

URL: www.benaturallycurious.com/airplane-printables/

password: **lift**

Table of Contents

Required materials: a Ping-Pong ball, two small paper cups, a penny, two straws, water, blow-dryer (optional), paper, scissors, tape measure, paper clips, two plastic bottles

Want to Be a Pilot?

Are you ready to fly? Come on! Jump in the cockpit, grab the controls, and let's go!!

You have your pilot's license—right? No? Well, then, not so fast. We'll need to learn some flight basics and have a good understanding of airplane science and **AERODYNAMICS** before we take off.

My name is Anna, and I'll be your flight instructor. Welcome to flight school!

Let's start by looking closely at the air.

Wave your arms around. Do you feel the air pushing on you? Air may be invisible, but there are molecules all around us (including oxygen, nitrogen, and carbon dioxide) that push back when you move. With the right conditions, air is strong enough to lift airplanes into the sky!

Let's add some motion. Have you ever stuck your arm out the window of a traveling car and felt the air move your arm? Now you can start to imagine the power of moving air. What happens when you tilt your hand in different directions? You feel a push against your hand—right? The push is a **FORCE**; it "forces" your arm to move in a certain direction.

> **A**erodynamics* is the study of airflow and how it affects moving objects.

> **A** *force* is a push or pull that causes a change.

Use caution when you hold your arm out of a window. Make sure there is nothing nearby that you could hit!

* Aero is Greek for "air"; dunamis or dynamis is the ancient Greek word for "power" or "force."

Airplanes are affected by four main forces. These forces work in opposite directions: up and down, forward and backward.

Let's look at each of these forces. Hold out your arms in a T-shape. Do you feel the pull down? The force of GRAVITY causes our arms to tire and also causes things to drop. An airplane needs to overcome the force of gravity to fly!

The next force is DRAG. Drag is the backward force that is opposite of the direction of flight. When you're holding your arm out the window of a car, you can create drag by positioning your hand with a flat palm vertical to the ground. The standard tube shape of an airplane aims to reduce the drag.

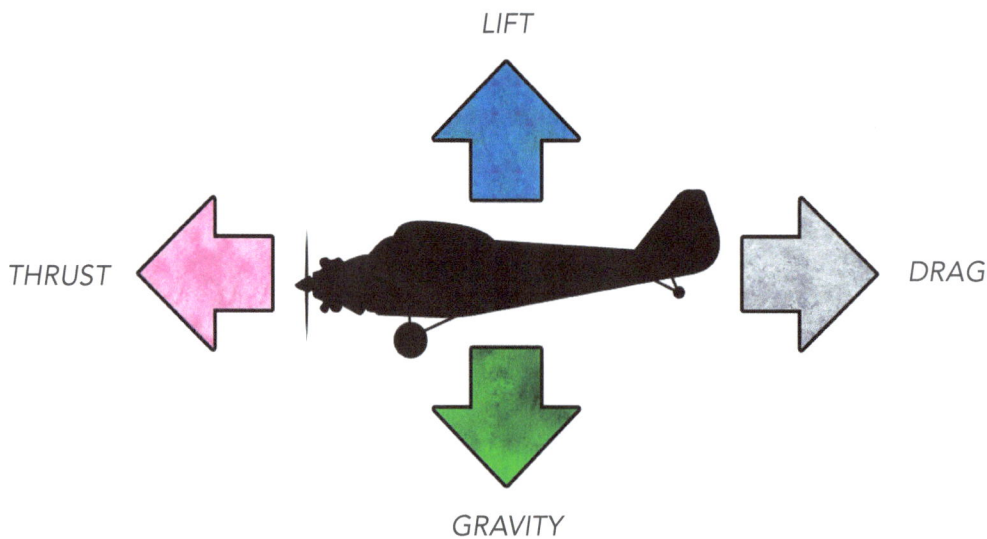

LIFT

THRUST

DRAG

GRAVITY

THRUST is a force going forward in the direction of flight. Thrust is created by engines— either propellers or jets. Propellers work better for planes that fly low and slow. Jets produce more thrust. They are used by airplanes that fly faster and at higher altitudes.

ALTITUDE *is the height or distance upward (measured from sea level or the ground).*

And … which direction haven't we talked about yet?

Up! The upward force that is so important for flight is called LIFT. Lift is created by the design of the airplane (in particular, the shape of the wings) combined with the forward motion created by the propellers or jets.

The four *forces* of flight are *thrust, drag, gravity* (or weight), and *lift.*

Let's create some lift! Hold a piece of paper in front of your mouth and just below it. Notice how the paper bends down to touch your chest. Now blow a gentle, steady stream of air over the paper. Do you see how the paper lifts up? Why did that happen?

Remember how we talked about the invisible air around us being full of molecules (such as oxygen, nitrogen, and carbon dioxide)? Your breath made the molecules in the air above the paper move faster than the air under the paper. The molecules under the paper, moving slower, push up. They put **PRESSURE** on the paper, and this pressure lifted the paper.

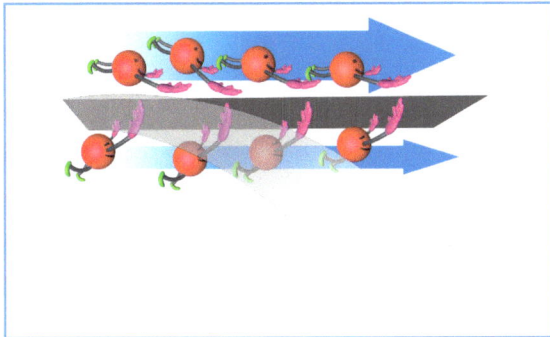

More molecules pushing create higher pressure under the paper.

Pressure is a force from the air molecules pushing against a surface.

Take your hand and make it flat. Are airplane wings flat like this?

Now cup your hand so there is a curve on the top. Airplane wings are designed like this, with a curved shape. When air molecules flow around this curved wing, they move faster above the wing than below the wing, similar to how the air moved faster above the paper when you blew over it. The slower-moving air under the airplane wing exerts pressure upward—enough to lift a huge 747 passenger plane!

Airplane wings, propellers, and even the tail of an airplane have this kind of curved shape that bends the air in just the right way. This design is called an **AIRFOIL**.

An *airfoil* is a surface with a curved shape that creates lift with airflow.

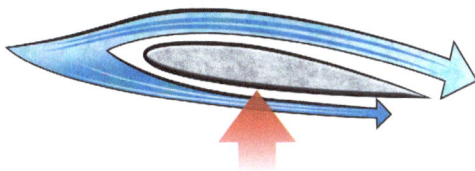

The effect of air movement around an airfoil is described as BERNOULLI'S PRINCIPLE, named after Jacob Bernoulli, a Swiss scientist who made his observations in 1738. In simple terms, Bernoulli's principle states that as the speed of air over a surface increases, the pressure decreases.

> Bernoulli's principle states that as the speed of air over a surface increases, the pressure decreases.

Now that you understand an airfoil and the basics of aerodynamics, it's time to learn to control the plane.

Getting a pilot's license is much more complicated than getting a driver's license for a car. While a car can move forward and backward, left and right, an airplane can go up and down, and even roll around like a corkscrew on a roller coaster!

The movement of an airplane in three-dimensional space is controlled with movable flaps.

AILERONS are the flaps on the wings. They allow the pilot to roll an airplane during flight. Imagine a pole through the front of an airplane that comes out the back. The airplane can move around this axis (stunt planes can even go upside down).

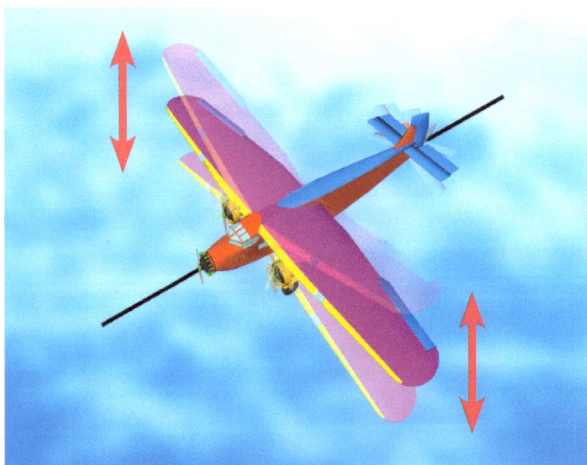

ROLL

> Ailerons control the rolling motion (roll) of the airplane.

The **RUDDER** on the trailing edges of the tail controls the left and right turning action, also called the **YAW**. Imagine a pole through the top of the plane pointing down to the ground and up to the sky. The rotation around this axis is the yaw.

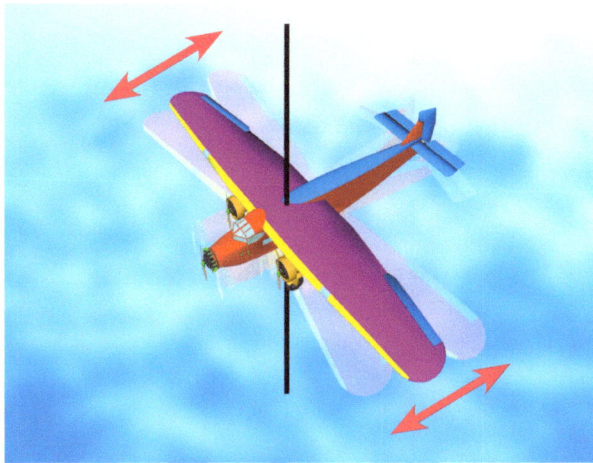

YAW

The *rudder* controls the right and left turning motion (*yaw*) of the airplane.

One more thing. The movement of the **ELEVATORS**, located on the tail, affect the pitch of the plane's nose—up to the sky or down toward the runway. Imagine a pole that goes through the wings and controls this horizontal axis.

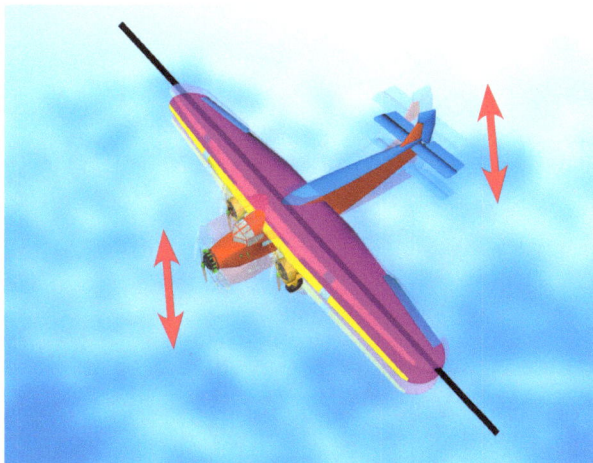

PITCH

Elevators control the up-and-down position of the nose (*pitch*) of the airplane.

Now that you know the different flight controls, you can imagine putting them together to fly the plane.

Great job and congratulations! You've completed the basics of flight school—a start toward a future pilot's license.

This is Instructor Anna signing off. Now it's time for you to do some experimentation with air pressure and the forces of airplane flight. Good luck and keep your eyes on the sky!

ACTIVITY
1

Playing with Air Pressure

We learned from Anna, our flight instructor, about Bernoulli's Principle:
"As the speed of air over a surface increases, the pressure decreases."
Let's play with this concept with some simple experiments.

EXPERIMENT 1

Preparation

1. Place two cups 6 inches apart, one in front of the other, on a table.

2. Place the Ping-Pong ball in the cup closer to the edge of the table.

MATERIALS

- Ping-Pong ball
- Two small paper cups
- A penny
- Two straws
- Water, blow-dryer (optional)

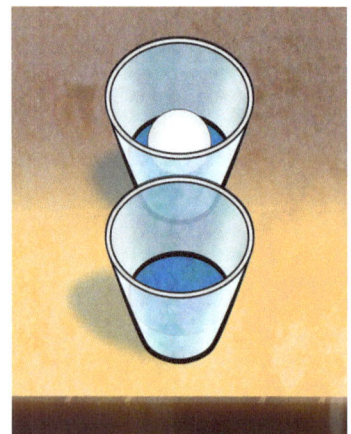

Challenge

- Using what you know about air pressure, try to figure out a way to get the ball from one cup to the other without using your hands.

    Hint: Blow across the top of the cup with the ball in it and watch it jump! Try to catch the ball in the other cup.

- Why does this happen?

    The air pressure moving across the top of the cup is lower than the pressure inside the cup. The higher pressure inside the cup forces the Ping-Pong ball out of the cup.

- Experiment with the distance between the two cups. Also, try the experiment with other lightweight objects.

ACTIVITY
1

Playing with Air Pressure

(continued)

EXPERIMENT 2

Preparation

1. Place a penny 2 inches from the edge of a table.

2. Hold a cup 2 inches beyond the penny with the opening of the cup toward the penny, slightly tilted up.

3. Cut a straw in half to make a "blower."

Challenge

• Using what you know about air pressure, try to figure out a way to get the penny into the cup without touching it.

  Hint: Blow one strong breath over the penny with the straw "blower."

• How does this happen?

  By blowing over the penny, you create low pressure, which causes the penny to jump.

• Try the experiment with different types of coins. Also, try the experiment with other lightweight objects.

EXPERIMENT 3

Preparation

1. Fill a cup with water and place one straw in the water.

2. Use the second straw, cut in half, as a "blower."

Challenge

• Using what you know about air pressure and what you have observed in the other experiments, what will happen when you blow across the top of the straw in the water?

ACTIVITY
1

Playing with Air Pressure

(continued)

Watch the water rise up in the straw due to the lower air pressure where the straws meet. The normal pressure of the water in the cup pushes the water up the straw.

• Experiment with different lengths of straws and different amounts of water. See if you can blow the water out the top of the straw. (Don't forget to clean up after yourself!)

EXPERIMENT 4

Preparation

1. Turn on a blow-dryer and point the air stream up.

2. Place the Ping-Pong ball on the air stream.

Challenge

• Explain how the flowing air creates lift.

The air flowing from the blow-dryer close to the ball is lower in pressure than the air away from the ball. The ball can balance there because the higher pressure of the air outside the flowing air pushes the ball back into the center.

• Experiment with the airflow. Turn it to different angles until the ball falls.

What are you CURIOUS about?

Let's Fly!

ACTIVITY 2

It's time to let it fly! You'll make a glider and test it, adjusting the elevators and rudder to make it go far and perform a controlled turn. Then get creative with some designs and additions of your own.

Preparation

1. Cut out the pattern on page 25 to make a dart glider (extra pattern sheets can be found on pages 27–31). Start with a fold down the center of the paper (line 1). Fold down along line 2 on each side. Continue with a fold down along line 3 on each side. Fold down along line 4. Finally, fold up along line 5 on each side.

2. To make the elevators and rudder, cut on the thick, solid lines and fold on the dotted lines.

3. Choose a starting line for the launch.

4. For each test flight, try to throw the glider the same:

   • height (shoulder or ear height is good)

   • launch angle (parallel to the ground, not tilted up or down)

   • speed (try flicking the wrist to throw)

5. Record your observations for each flight test in your Experimental Journal (page 23).

MATERIALS

• Paper

• Glider pattern from page 25 (extra glider patterns can be found on pages 27–31)

• Scissors

• Tape measure

• Heavy and lightweight paper (optional)

• Paper clips (optional)

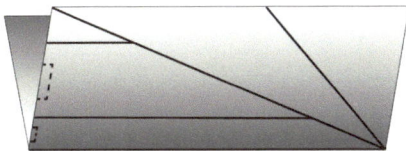

Fold along line 1

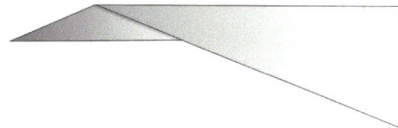

Fold along line 2

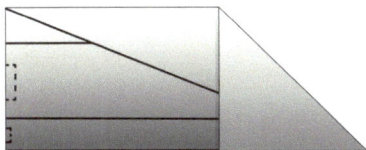

Fold along line 3

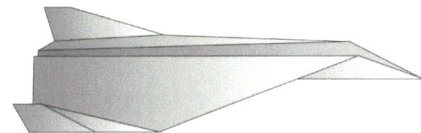

Fold along line 4

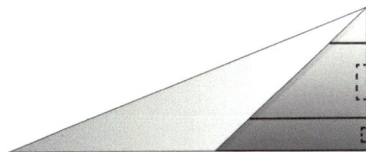

Fold along line 5

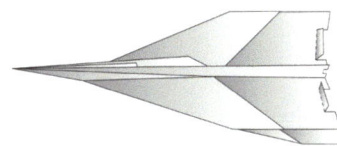

Cut on elevator and rudder lines

ACTIVITY
2

Let's Fly!

(continued)

EXPERIMENT 1: FLY THE FARTHEST

- Throw your glider. Observe how it flies.

- Record the flight distance and observations on the worksheet in the row labeled "Flight Test 1."

- Adjust your glider so it flies in a straight line.

- Now it's time to adjust the glider flaps and try to get the longest flight without it stalling, nose-diving, or turning. For each test flight, record the distance and adjustments on the worksheet. Here are some tips:

  - If the glider dives downward, turn up the back edges of the wings (elevators up).

  - If it pitches up, bend the back edges of the wings down (elevators down).

  - If the glider yaws to the right or left, turn the rudder in the opposite direction of the turn (and adjust the elevators so one is higher than the other).

  - If the plane rolls, adjust the angle of the wings so it's more of a V-shape rather than flat.

EXPERIMENT 2: MAKE A CONTROLLED TURN

- From what you observed in Experiment 1, adjust your glider so it will turn to the left. Mark a goal for your flight and try to get your glider to land where you want it to (a hula hoop, bucket, or X on the ground is a good target).

- Adjust the glider to reach a goal to the right of the launch line.

CHALLENGE: DESIGN YOUR OWN GLIDER!

Make another glider with a different kind of paper. How does lighter or heavier paper affect flight? Add a paper clip along the body of the glider. How does weight affect the flight?

Pressure Pop

We learned from our flight instructor, Anna, that *pressure* is very important to flight—it's what creates *lift*! Also important in airplane science is that as you go up in *altitude*, pressure decreases (gets lower).

When an airplane travels above 12,500 feet, it's necessary to control the cabin pressure to make sure the passengers and crew are comfortable and safe.

Have you ever had your ears "pop" in an airplane, driving on a mountain road, or in the elevator of a very tall building? Our ears "pop" because of pressure differences.

As we change altitude, the air spaces in our inner ears need to have the same pressure as the air around us; in other words, the air pressure needs to equalize. The "pop" happens when the tiny tubes between the inner and outer ears open up. Then the air pressure is equalized. (Tip: To make your ears pop, keep your face and jaw muscles moving by yawning, swallowing, or chewing on something.)

Although the moving air molecules that create pressure are invisible, it's possible to see the effects of changing air pressure by experimenting with two plastic bottles.

INSTRUCTIONS

1. Choose one bottle as the "control." (That means you observe what happens without changing anything during the experiment.) Label this one Bottle 1.

2. Label the other one Bottle 2. This will be the experimental bottle.

3. When you are on the ground (or at the base of the mountain), tighten the caps of both bottles.

4. Think about what might happen to the bottles as you change altitude. Record your thoughts on the worksheet as your hypotheses. Very simply, a hypothesis is what you think will happen.

MATERIALS

- Two plastic bottles
- A trip where you can experience a pressure difference (airplane travel, mountain road, and/or tall elevator)

Pressure Pop

INSTRUCTIONS (continued)

5. When you reach your highest altitude, observe what happened to Bottle 1 and record it on the worksheet.

6. At this high altitude, remove the cap from Bottle 2 to equalize the pressure inside and outside the bottle. Put the cap back on Bottle 2. Remember that Bottle 1 is the control, so don't do anything to it.

7. When you are back on the ground at low altitude, look at Bottles 1 and 2, and record your observations in your Experimental Journal (pages 33 and 35). How did your observations line up with your hypotheses?

What are you CURIOUS about?

ACTIVITY
4

Animal Flight Matching Game

Airplanes are not the only things that encounter the four forces of flight. Birds, bats, and bugs have spent millions of years perfecting the science of flight. Some animals have learned to glide to help them move around in their habitat (natural setting) and find food.

This game will challenge you to think about where these flying and gliding animals live, what they eat, and the kinds of wing shapes and flying styles that help them survive.

INSTRUCTIONS

Preparation

1. Cut out the Animal and Flight cards.

2. Spread out the Animal cards face down on one side of the table.

3. Spread out the Flight cards face down on the other side of the table.

Playing the Game

1. Player 1 turns over an Animal card and then turns over a Flight card.

2. Player 1 reads the Flight card and sees if the description matches the animal (check the Answer Key if it's not clear).

3. If the two cards match, Player 1 gets to keep both cards and takes another turn.

4. If the two cards don't match, Player 1 turns both cards face down again (remembering where they are!).

5. Then Player 2 chooses one card from each side, trying to make a match.

6. The game continues until all the cards are matched up.

7. The player with the most cards wins!

> ### MATERIALS
> - Copies of the Animal and Flight game cards (pages 37 and 39)
> - Scissors
> - Answer Key, page 18

ACTIVITY
4

Animal Flight Matching Game

INSTRUCTIONS (continued)

Study this guide of four common types of bird wings to help you think about how different wing shapes help these animals fly. Some bird wings fall in between these general groups.

Wing shape	Kind of flight	Examples
very long, narrow	gliding for long distances using air currents for lift	albatrosses, gulls, and gannets
broad, slotted feathers	soaring, climbing upward currents of warm air	eagles, hawks, herons, and storks
short, round (elliptical)	short bursts of speed; good for the forest	crows, robins, blackbirds, and sparrows; also bats
long, thin	high-speed, long distance	swifts, ducks, falcons, terns, and sandpipers

Answer Key

Animal	Flight Card
Owl	1
Pigeon	2
Albatross	3
Hawk	4
Hummingbird	5
Gull	6
Flying fish	7
Bat	8
Flying squirrel	9
Dragonfly	10
Housefly	11
Ladybug	12

Curiosity Connector

Here are some links to help you follow your curiosity!

- Build more paper airplanes. This link includes videos to help you fold them:
  www.paperaeroplanes.com

- To take it to the next level, try this solar-powered, phone-controlled paper plane:
  www.diydrones.com/profiles/blogs/iphone-controlled-paper-airplane

- Learn more about pitch, yaw, and roll flight controls at:
  www.youngeagles.org/games/pyr

- Check out these fun activities about flight:
  http://howthingsfly.si.edu/

- Try this simple flight simulator to control an airplane:
  http://howthingsfly.si.edu/activities/controlled-flight

- Or simulate a flight with Google Earth:
  1. Download Google Earth at www.Earth.google.com
  2. Go to "Tools," then choose "Flight simulator."
  3. Learn the keyboard controls or plug in a joystick to fly.

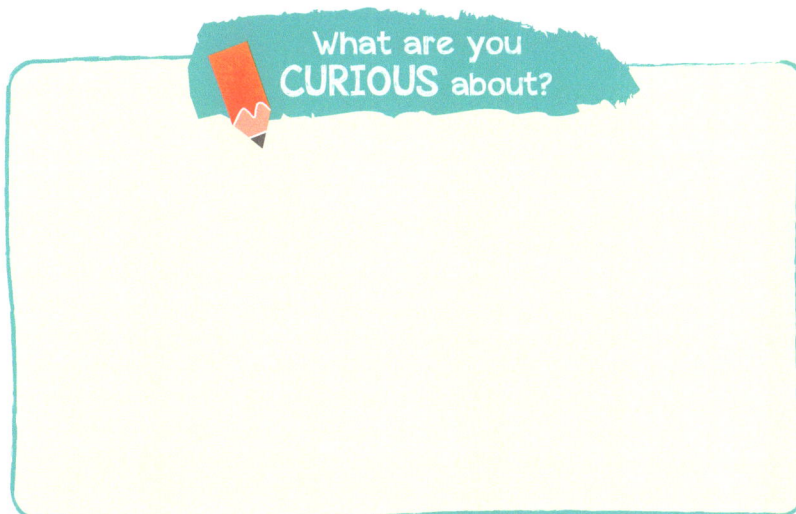

What are you CURIOUS about?

Airport Extras

Will you be flying in a passenger airplane before long? Here are some ideas for learning more about airplane science while you're traveling.

- When making airline reservations, choose a window seat just behind the wings so you can watch the flaps move. During the flight, watch to see if water forms on the wings (due to lower pressure above, which makes water changes from a gas to a solid).

- Ask to visit the pilots in the cockpit. Ask them to point out some of the controls that move the flaps.

- Look at the shapes of the different airplanes around the airport. Look for the airfoil shape of the wings. Observe where the propellers or jets are located on different airplanes.

Tools for Your Tool Kit

Let's make the ideas you learned today part of your life tool kit. Remember to print out some blank tool kit pages and tape or glue on today's tools.

1. The force created from air molecules pushing against a surface is _____ .

   Add **PRESSURE** to your tool kit.

2. A surface with a curved shape that creates lift with airflow is an _____ .

   Add **AIRFOIL** to your tool kit.

3. What is the upward force that an airplane needs in order to fly? _____ .

   Add **LIFT** to your tool kit.

4. Match the flaps with how they control the airplane:

AILERONS	ROLL (side to side)
RUDDER	PITCH (up and down)
ELEVATOR	YAW (right and left)

   Add **FLIGHT CONTROLS** to your tool kit!

Glossary

AERODYNAMICS – the study of airflow and how it affects moving objects

AILERONS – the flaps on airplane wings that control the side-to-side motion (roll)

AIRFOIL – a surface with a curved shape that creates lift with airflow

ALTITUDE – the height or distance up from a reference point, such as sea level or the ground

BERNOULLI'S PRINCIPLE – a law of physics establishing that as the speed of air over a surface increases, the pressure decreases

DRAG – a force that resists motion and pulls an airplane backward

ELEVATORS – flaps that control the up-and-down position (pitch) of the airplane nose

FORCE – a push or pull that causes a change

GRAVITY – a force that pulls objects downward toward Earth's surface

LIFT – an upward force

PRESSURE – the force from air molecules pushing against a surface

RUDDER – the flap on an airplane that controls the right and left turning (yaw)

THRUST – a forward force, in the direction of flight, that is created by the propellers or jets on an airplane

YAW – the right and left turning motion of an airplane

ACTIVITY 2

Experimental Journal

EXPERIMENT 1 – FLY THE FARTHEST

Flight Test	Distance Flown	Flight Observations	Adjustments for Next Flight Test
1			
2			
3			
4			
5			

EXPERIMENT 2 – MAKE A CONTROLLED TURN

Flight Test	Flight Observations	Adjustments for Next Flight Test
1		
2		
3		
4		
5		

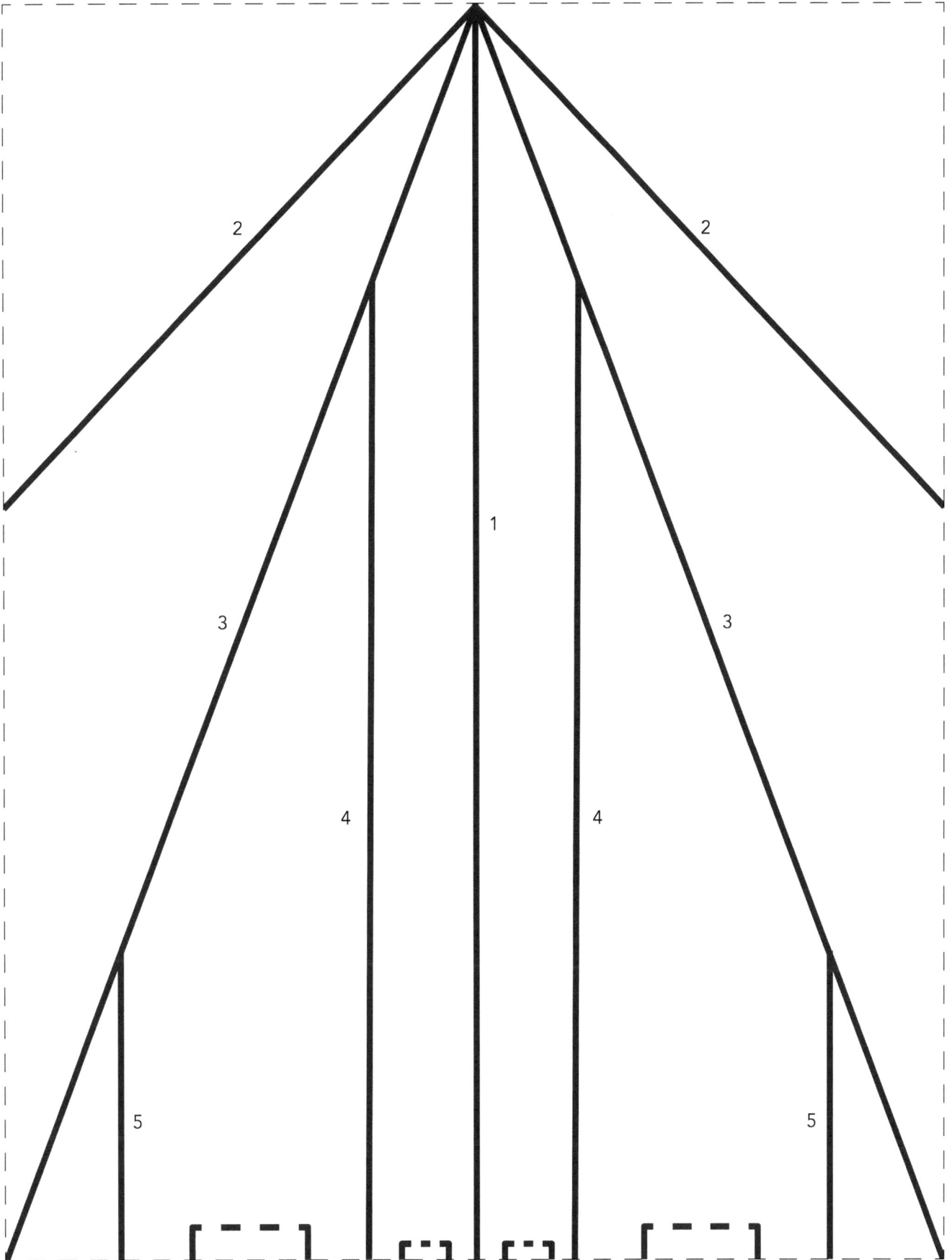

2

2

1

3

3

4

4

5

5

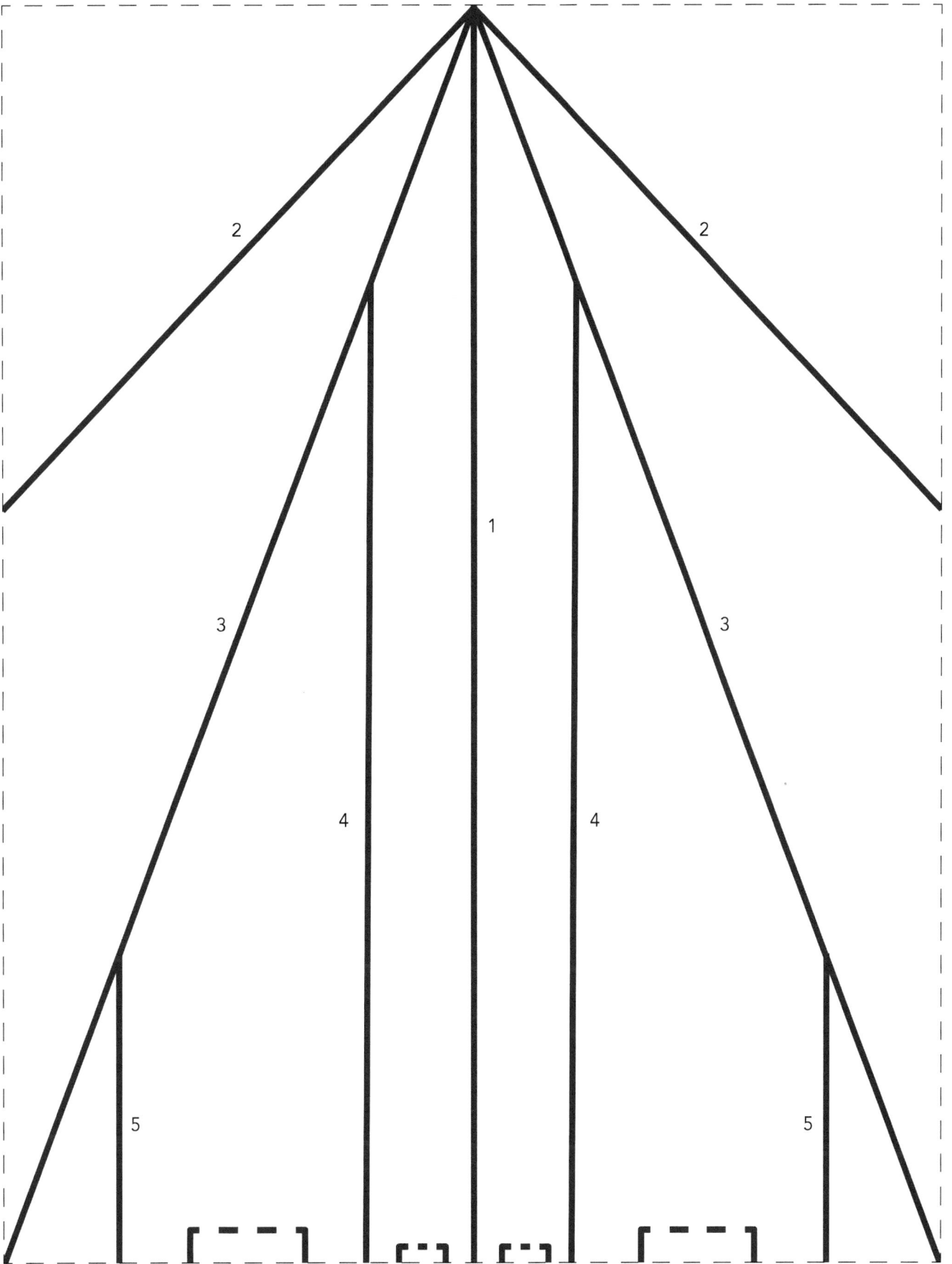

2

2

3

1

3

4

4

5

5

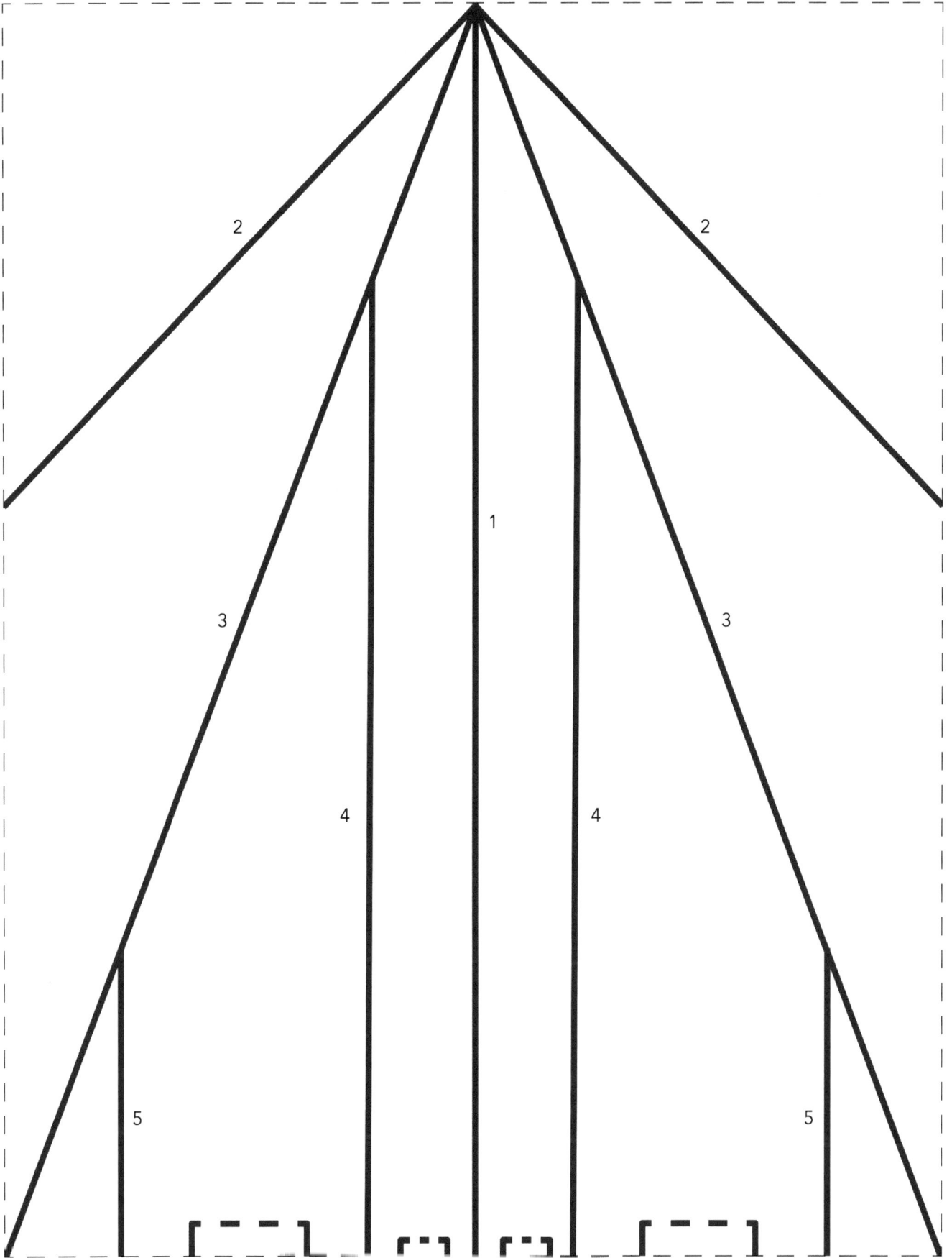

2

2

1

3

3

4

4

5

5

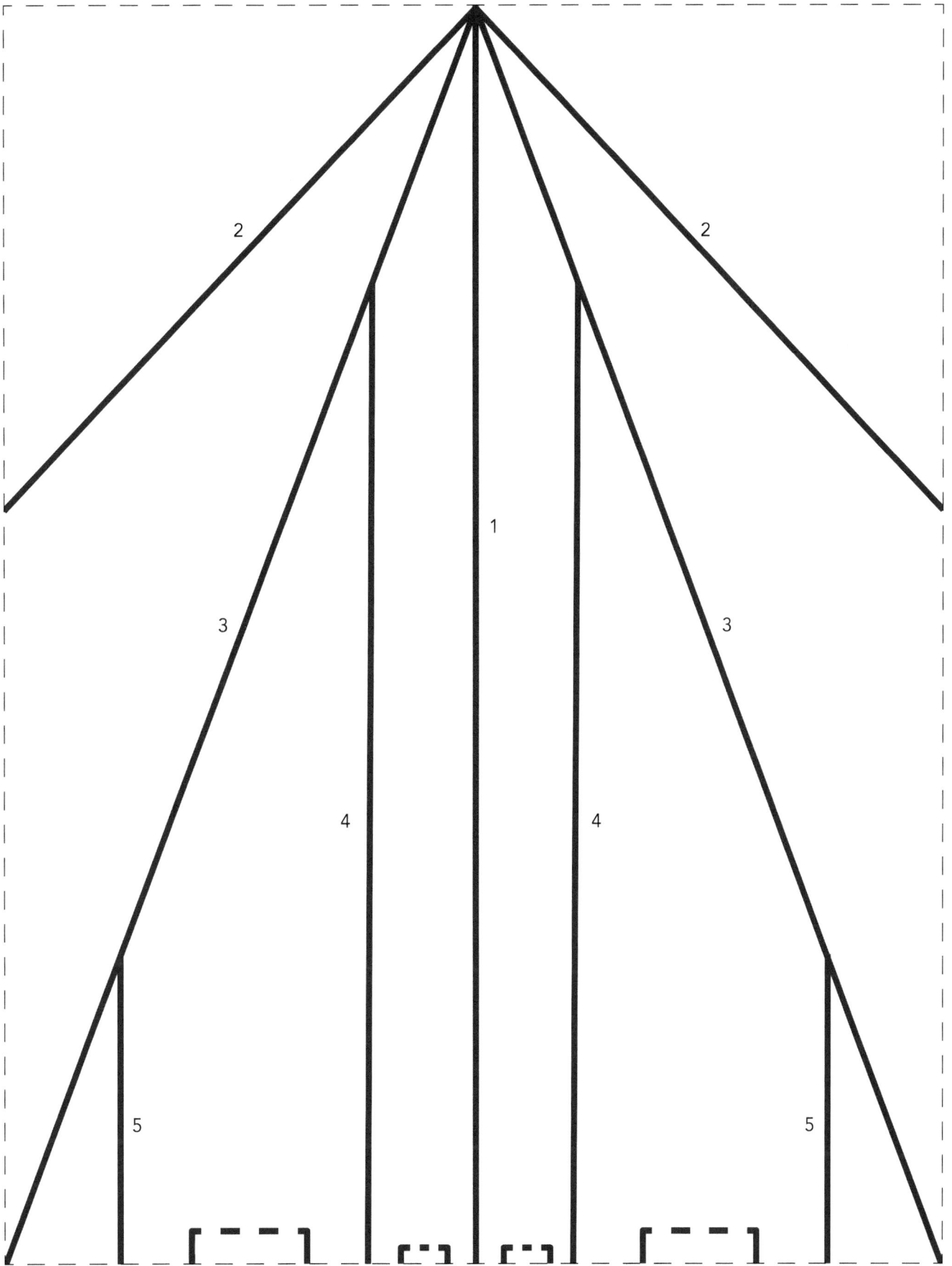

2

2

1

3

3

4

4

5

5

ACTIVITY 3

Experimental Journal

VARIATION 1: IN AN AIRPLANE

BOTTLE 1 (Cap stays on the whole time.)	Hypothesis (what you think will happen)	Observations
At cruising altitude		
Back on the ground		

BOTTLE 2 (Cap is removed and then replaced at high altitude.)	Hypothesis (what you think will happen)	Observations
At cruising altitude (after removing the cap, but before replacing it)		
Back on the ground		

ACTIVITY 3

Experimental Journal

VARIATION 2: DRIVING ON A MOUNTAIN ROAD OR IN AN ELEVATOR

BOTTLE 1 (Cap stays on the whole time.)	Hypothesis (what you think will happen)	Observations
At high altitude		
Back at low altitude		

BOTTLE 2 (Cap is removed and then replaced at high altitude.)	Hypothesis (what you think will happen)	Observations
At high altitude (after removing the cap but before replacing it)		
Back at low altitude		

Cutouts for Activity 4: Animal Flight Matching Game

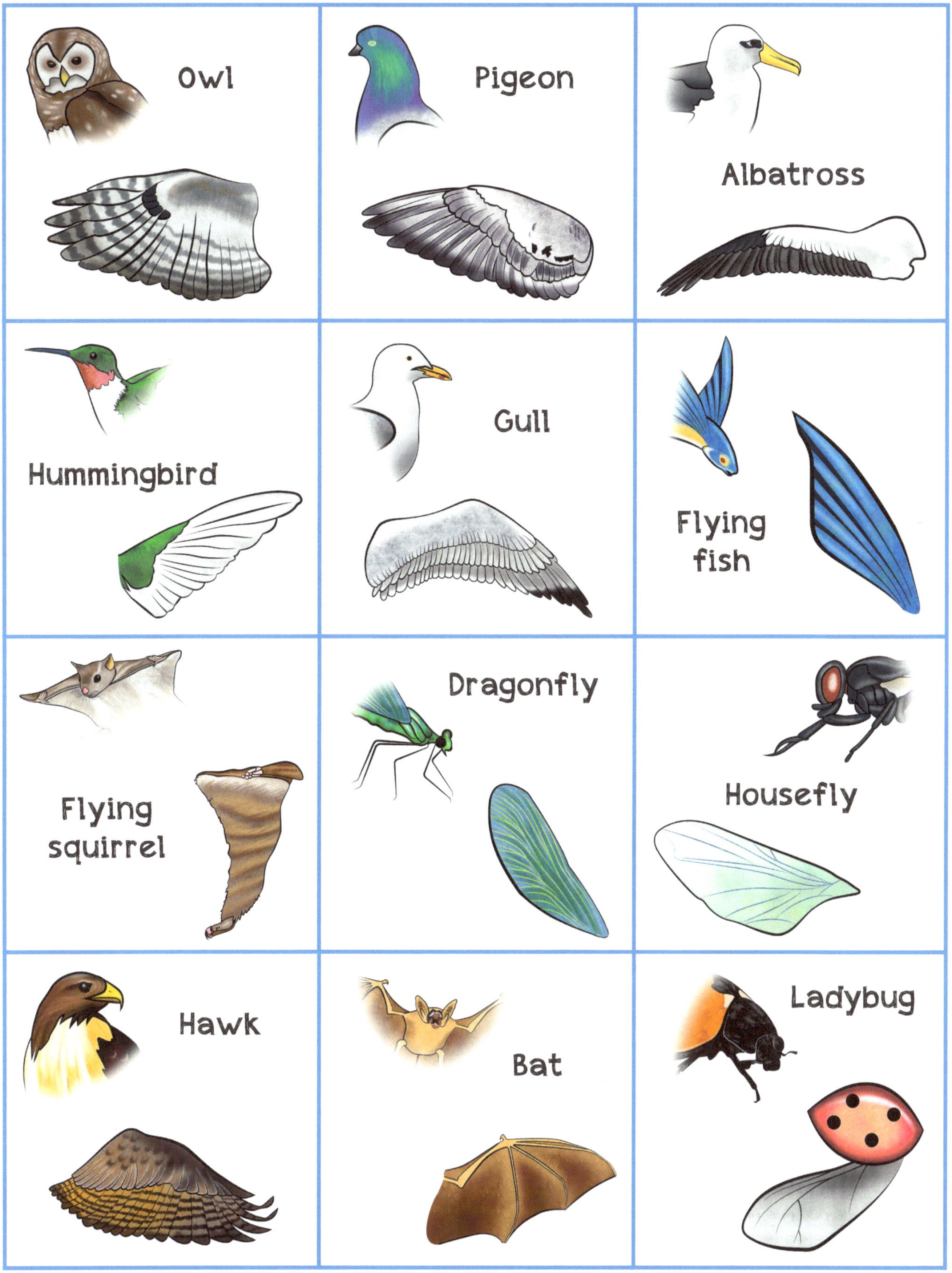

Owl
Pigeon
Albatross
Hummingbird
Gull
Flying fish
Flying squirrel
Dragonfly
Housefly
Hawk
Bat
Ladybug

1

Wings: broad

Flight: silent, swooping

Habitat: forest, fields

Food: small animals

2

Wings: short, round

Flight: fast, short-distance

Habitat: city, urban

Food: seeds, bugs

3

Wings: long, narrow

Flight: gliding

Habitat: open ocean

Food: fish

4

Wings: broad

Flight: soaring

Habitat: open fields

Food: small animals

5

Wings: narrow

Flight: hovering

Habitat: where there are flowers (but only in the Americas!)

Food: flower nectar

6

Wings: narrow, thin

Flight: gliding

Habitat: shoreline

Food: fish, shellfish, bugs

7

Wings: fins (not true wings)

Flight: gliding (not true flying)

Habitat: ocean

Food: small fish, plankton

8

Wings: broad, stretched skin

Flight: quick flapping

Habitat: many different

Food: bugs, nectar, or fish

9

Wings: stretched skin (not true wings)

Flight: gliding (not a true flyer)

Habitat: forest

Food: nuts, seeds

10

Wings: 4 long, narrow wings

Flight: darting

Habitat: near fresh water

Food: bugs

11

Wings: 2 long wings, 2 small rudders (called halteres)

Flight: fast, short-distance

Habitat: house

Food: garbage, human food

12

Wings: 2 wings under 2 protective shields (called elytra)

Flight: buzzing

Habitat: gardens, near plants

Food: bugs, aphids

Science Tool Kit

www.ingramcontent.com/pod-product-compliance
Lightning Source LLC
LaVergne TN
LVHW072131070426
835513LV00002B/57